Chess for Kids

Learn in 30 Minutes a Day

By: Activity Nest

activitynest.org

This book is dedicated to the children of the world. May your hearts be full of joy.
If you enjoy the book, please consider leaving a review wherever you bought it.

Table of Contents

Introduction to Chess

What game do you have the most fun playing? A video game? An outdoor game?

There is a game that is so much fun that it became popular everywhere it went. It's a game that is so old that it used to be called "The Game of Kings" because powerful kings enjoyed playing it when they weren't ruling their kingdoms. You don't have to be a king to play it today. In fact, it's probably sitting in your closet right now, waiting for a special kid like you to come along and dust it off.

That game is chess.

Chess is so much fun that it will actually make you smarter and help you see things in different and special ways. When you learn to play chess, you will always have someone to play with. There are clubs for people who play chess, and there's probably one in your school right now! So where did chess come from, then?

History of Chess

Chess is a very old game -- at least 1,500 years old. Most people think that it started in the North of India, but nobody knows for sure. It moved through Persia and into the Islamic world, where it was carried to other parts of Europe and Asia. Wherever chess went, it became popular. The rules changed a lot up until the 1880s. This was a very special time for chess, where the rules didn't change much, and people became madly in love with the game. Regular tournaments started to become common, and unique chess clocks were invented.

Here we are today, where very smart computers can help us learn or play chess if we don't have anyone to play with. Games are recorded and preserved for studying later. You can do the same with your own games if you want.

Did you know that there were some kings that didn't like chess and didn't want anyone in their kingdom to play the game? People would play so much that some kings thought that the game was a waste of time and a big distraction, so they banned it. Chess was banned more than once throughout history. Now, the gameis far too popular to outlaw, so this is the best time in history to love chess. There are more ways to learn and more ways to practice than ever before. You're starting in the right place by reading this book.

Chess may look like a hard game, but it's actually very easy. Well, it's easy to learn how to play. You will spend the rest of your life learning how to get better and better, which will all be fun. You will find out that the more you play, the smarter you get, and the more you look at things differently. Yes, chess is very good for your brain.

Setting up the board

Have you ever seen a chessboard? It's a black and white checkerboard of 64 squares. It looks very much like a game of checkers, but there are a few special differences.

Look at the picture above. There's a right way and a wrong way to have the board when you play chess. First, there must be a white square in the lower right-hand corner of the board. Write a "W" with a pen on your right hand if that helps you remember. *White on the right.*

The second difference is what you see on the sides. Do you see the numbers one through eight and the letters A through H? This is what lets us keep track of moves so we can save the games we play forever. We'll see how to do this later.

The rows of squares that go up and down with the letters A through H are called *files.*

The rows of squares that go side to side with the numbers 1 through 8 are called *ranks.*

Here is what the board looks like when all the pieces are in place.

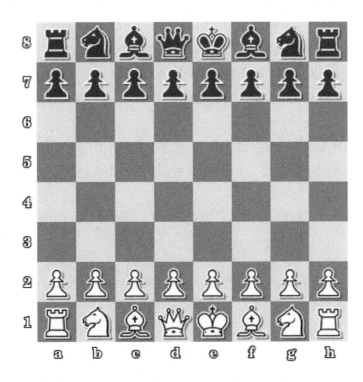

Does it look confusing? Don't worry. You'll know how to set the board up in your sleep when you're done with this book.

Notice that the white pieces always start in ranks 1 and 2, and the black pieces always start in ranks 7 and 8.

The Chessmen and How They Move

Have you ever played with plastic soldiers? That's what the chess pieces are; soldiers. You have Footmen with spears, archers with arrows, and knights on horses. Unlike plastic toy soldiers, your chessmen will do real battle! Let's look at each one and learn who they are, how they move, and how they attack.

The Pawn

One square at a time in a straight line. If I'm blocked, I'm locked.

He's super-brave and super-small. There's a lot of him. He's the pawn. Pawns line up in front of all your other chessmen. The pawn has stayed the same from the earliest versions of chess. They represent soldiers that fight face-to-face. They've often been shown as fighters with spears or other long pole weapons. It makes sense when you see how they attack. Read on to find out.

It's true that the pawn is the weakest character in the game, but don't be fooled. Pawns can be very useful, and you'll get to see why later on.

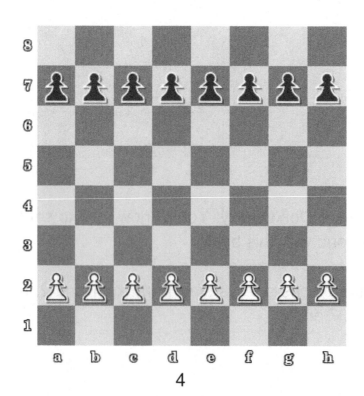

4

Behold, the brave and mighty pawn! Standing in front of the line of fire with no protection! It's too bad that the pawn can only move one square at a time, and unlike his friends, he cannot move backward. Ever.

The pawn has a chance to move *two squares forward*, and it's on the pawn's very first movement. In the picture below, any of the black's pawns can move two squares forward if they want since none of them has moved yet. White's pawns have all moved, so they can only move one square at a time for the rest of the game.

In the next picture, two pawns are right up against each other. Maybe they're talking about the weather or perhaps they're eating a ham sandwich. Whatever they're doing, they'll be there for a while. If a pawn has something directly in front of it, then that pawn is blocked and will not be able to move.

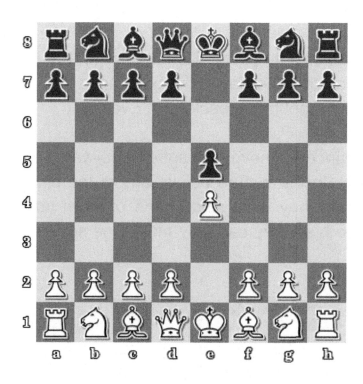

So are pawns just going for a walk on the board, or can they actually attack? Yes, they can. But only if there's something in a square ahead of them diagonally. Pretend that the pawn holds a long spear across his chest for protection, but a slight swing of either end can swipe at the squares diagonally placed from him.

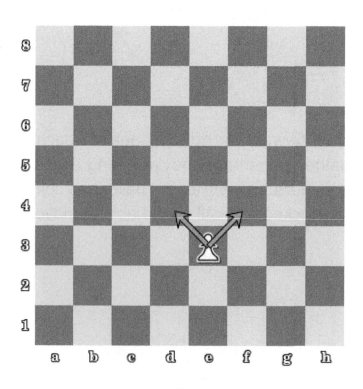

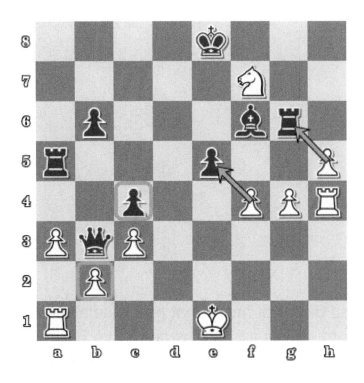

So why bother moving pawns if they're so slow? If a pawn makes it all the way to the other end of the board, then it becomes very, very powerful. You'll find out about that in a bit.

The King

The king is by far the most important piece on the board. When the king can no longer move without being attacked, the game ends. So it is your duty to protect the king at all costs. This isn't to say that the king should cower in the corner of the board for the entire battle. As the game wears on, the king becomes a very powerful fighter. But it's best to make sure that he always has a few bodyguards.

His highness can only move one square at a time. The good news is that he can move in any direction he wants as long as there are empty squares and nobody attacking.

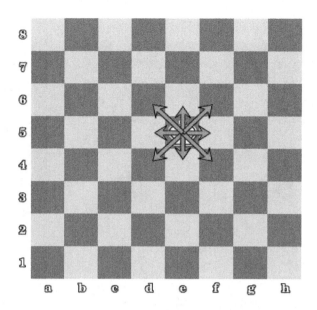

The king's slow speed does not mean that he is useless or helpless. The old king swings a mighty sword, and many chessmen have underestimated his strength and his bravery in battle. You don't live long enough to become king by being a coward.

The Queen

I go where I want, and I move in eight lines! There's no use in hiding. If I see you, you're mine!

Once upon a time, there weren't any girls on the chessboard. The queen used to be a counselor or prime minister to the king. He could only move one square at a time diagonally. The royal lady we know and love today came to be around the 15th century. The way she moves is, well, just look below.

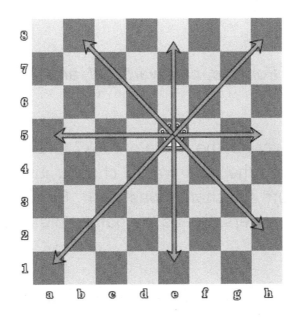

The queen is by far the most powerful piece on the board. She carries a frying pan and can throw it however far she needs to at anyone who laughs at her. Forward and backward, left or right, and even diagonally! No wonder many chess players protect their queen almost as much as they protect their king! Although it is possible to win the game without the queen. Some very clever wins were made by giving up the queen to make it look like they were losing!

None are safe from the power of the queen!

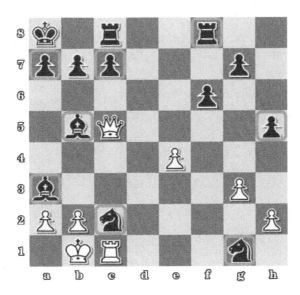

The white queen threatens all of the pieces marked in blue.

The Rook

In four directions, I fight. Forward, backward, left, and right. Like a cannon, I blast if you're in sight.

How did a little castle tower get the name of rook? It has to do with what the rook was in Persia. Back then, the rook was a chariot, just like the kind driven by horses. The Persian word for chariot was **rukh**. See? Those ancient armored chariots looked a bit like towers. So, as the game spread, the rook became more like a castle.

Your rooks are very powerful pieces. Weaker than the queen, but overall stronger than bishops and knights. You can see why they're like chariots, or even like cannons! They can move forward and backward, left or right, any number of squares if there's nothing blocking their path.

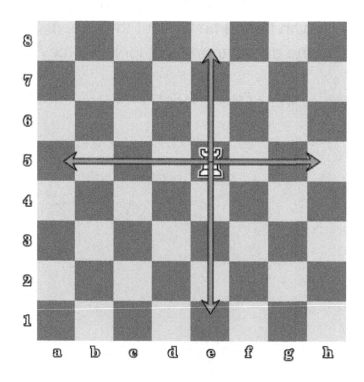

The Bishop

One on a dark square, one on light. I fire sharp arrows down diagonal lines.

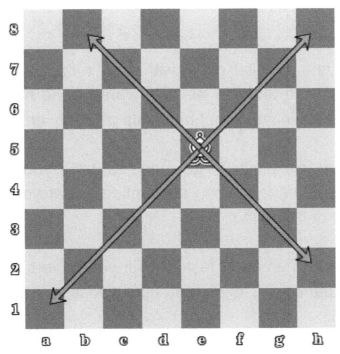

Think of the bishop as an archer. It's able to move as many squares as it wants along diagonal lines, which means that the color of the square that the bishop starts out on is the color of the square that it stays on for the rest of the game.

A bishop that starts out on a dark square will always be on a dark square for the rest of the game, and the same goes for the other bishop that starts on a white square. The bishop with his pointed miter hat was, once upon a time, not the bishop in chess.

The game that chess evolved out of actually had the bishop as an elephant; which reflects the culture that Chess came out of in the beginning. The bishop/elephant used to be very slow, too. It still moves in a diagonal line, but it could only move two squares at a time diagonally. So, in order to speed up the game, the bishop was allowed to move in as many squares as possible if there was a clear path to do so.

The Knight

I leap and fly and make scaredy-cats cry. I always have eight squares under my eye. Two-one is the way I glide—two squares North, South, East, or West, and then one to the side.

The knight in chess is a peculiar piece with even more peculiar movements. He has the head of the horse and the will of a warrior, and he's able to dance and prance over his enemies in ways that his rivals can only envy.

He's probably the hardest piece to get used to, so if you get used to knowing how the knight moves, then you can be confident that you're going to become very good at the rest of the game.

The knight moves in an L-shaped fashion. All you have to remember is that he can move forward, backward, or side-to-side two spaces and then forward or backward one space.

So if you move two squares forward, you move one square to the side, either left or right.

If you move two squares back, then you move one square to the side, left or right.

If you move two squares left, then you move one square, either up or down, and if you move two squares right, then you move one square up or down. Easy enough? Not really. Perhaps a diagram will help.

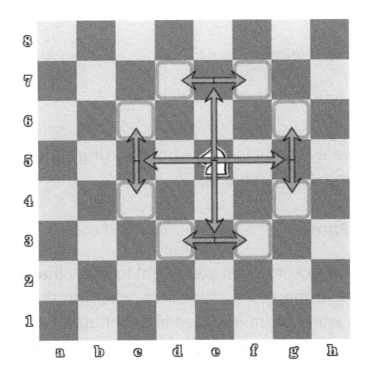

At any given time, the knight is able to move to eight squares around him, and you'll see how the L-shape can be made into the path that goes in those directions to those eight squares.

Even though the knight may be able to jump, he is not allowed to share a square with another piece. If there is a piece where he's trying to get to, he either captures it if it's an enemy piece or he simply can't move there if it's a piece of his own color. In fact, no two pieces ever share the same square in chess.

The knight is also like the pawn in that it hasn't changed much throughout the history of chess. The horseman has remained the horseman.

So Who's Keeping Score?

There's no way of keeping score or tallying points in chess. But there is a way of getting an idea who is ahead with numbers called Reinfeld Values. These numbers give you a general idea of how much worth of the enemy's pieces you've captured. They don't guarantee that anyone is winning, though. You can capture a large Reinfeld score and still lose. But the values do lend some perspective to the overall direction a game is headed.

Pawns = 1 point
Bishops and Knights = 3 points
Rooks = 5 points
Queen = 9 points

The king doesn't have a Reinfeld value since the king is never removed from the board. Without the king, the game ends.

The Goal of the Game

If you've ever played checkers, then you ought to know that the goal of the game is to completely remove the other player's checkers from the board. But this is not so in chess. The whole point of chess is to set up a position where the other king cannot move. This is done by either blocking the enemy king's path or creating squares that are under attack.

Look at the picture below. Do you still remember how a rook moves? That's right—Forward, backward, and side to side. The white king is not allowed to move into any of the squares that the rook could move to.

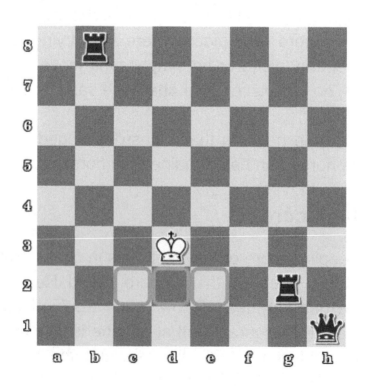

It's black's turn to move!

Uh oh. Black just put the white king in a threatened square. This is called check. When you move, and the other player's king is in a square your pieces could move to, you have to call out "Check!" The other player must remove the king from check either by moving the king from that square, blocking the attacking piece's path, or capturing the attacking piece.

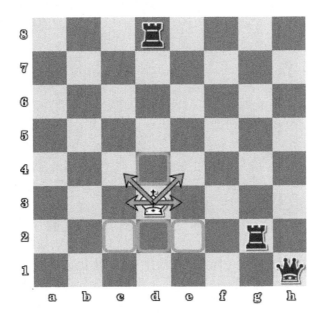

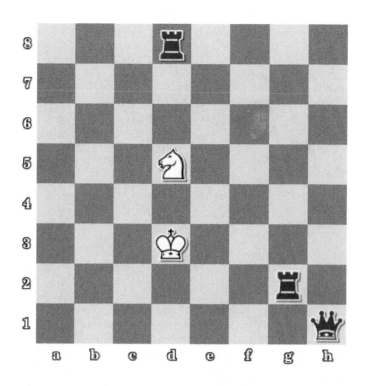

If white had other pieces on the board, they could be used to block the check.

Several moves later, we have this situation. Black moves and puts the king in check again!

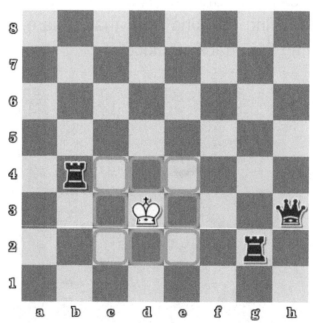

What can white do to get out of check? Uh oh. It looks like there's no way to get out of check this time.

If there's really no way to get the king out of check, then black has to call out "Checkmate!" and the game is over. Black wins. The goal of the game, then, is to get the other player's king in checkmate before they get your king into checkmate.

There are many, many different ways to score a checkmate. This is the part of chess that is considered an art. We'll look at a few checkmates from past games.

Donald Byrne vs. Robert James Fischer

1956

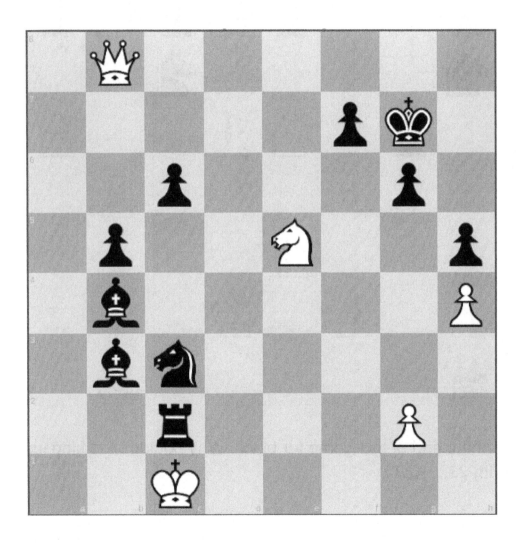

Robbie Fischer (black) made a stunning checkmate with **41...Rc2#.**
Do you see why the king can't move anywhere?

Adolf Anderssen vs Lionel Adalber Bagration Felix Kieseritzky

1851

Adolf Anderssen vs **Lionel Adalbert Bagration Felix Kieseritzky**
"The Immortal Game" (game of the day Sep-05-2007)
London (1851), London ENG, Jun-21
King's Gambit: Accepted. Bishop's Gambit Bryan Countergambit (C33) · 1-0

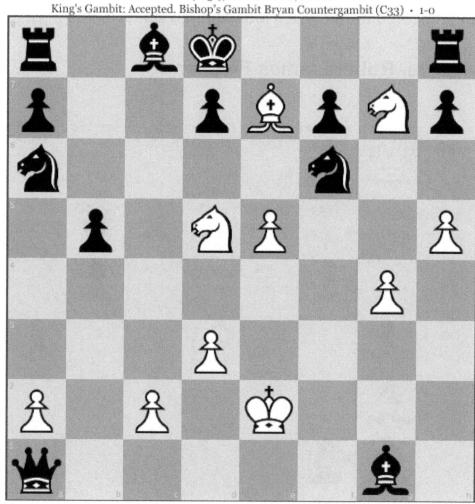

23. Be7# was the end of this game for black. Why couldn't the king just move out of danger with **23... Kc7?**

Paul Morphy vs. Duke Karl / Count Isouard

1858

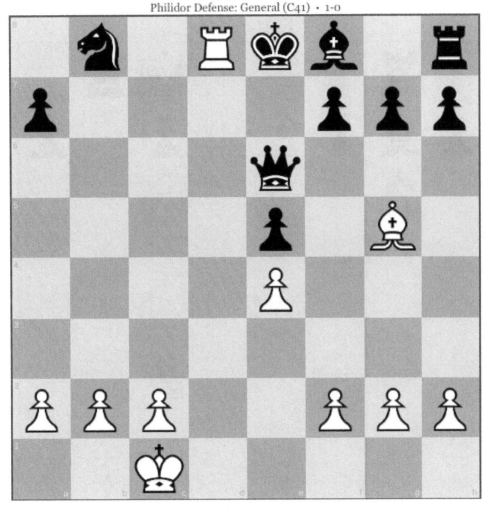

Paul Morphy vs Duke Karl / Count Isouard
"A Night at the Opera" (game of the day Dec-02-2007)
Paris (1858), Paris FRA
Philidor Defense: General (C41) · 1-0

17. Rd8# ends this rather old game from 1858. Notice how it doesn't take much to make a checkmate.

Adolf Anderssen vs Jean Dufresne

1852

Adolf Anderssen vs **Jean Dufresne**
"The Evergreen Partie" (game of the day Oct-16-2017)
Berlin (1852), Berlin GER
Italian Game: Evans Gambit. Pierce Defense (C52) · 1-0

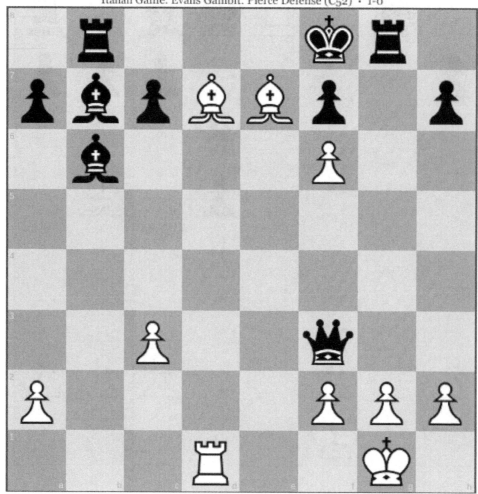

24. Bxe7# shows you that you can't underestimate the power of a pawn.

Special moves

There are a few special moves in chess that can only be done once or just a few times. These were rules that were introduced late in history and were mostly structured to speed up the game or to keep the game balanced. The first special move is **castling**.

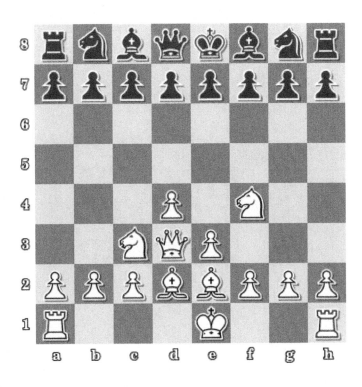

Castling is a defensive move that hastens the king to safety in a hurry. You don't have to castle, but it's helpful. Notice the king in the above diagram. All you have to do is pick a side you want to castle to. You can castle to the side of the board the king is already sitting on, which is called *castling kingside*, or you can castle to the other side of the board where the queen sits, which is called *castling queenside*.

To castle kingside, the king must not have moved yet since the beginning of the game. The squares between the king and the rook must be empty, and the rook must not have moved yet either.

To castle kingside, move the king two squares toward the rook and put the rook on the opposite side of the king. This castling is sometimes known as *castling short*; the rook moves a short distance (two squares).

21

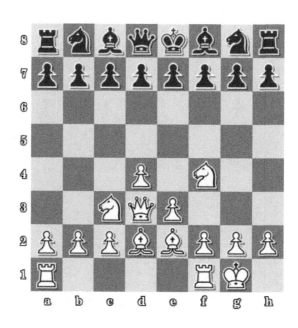

Castling Kingside

Castling to the queenside is very similar but looks a little lopsided. Just like before, this time, you also have to move the king two spaces to the side you're castling. Then you put the rook on the opposite side of the king. Looks kind of funny, doesn't it? It may not look right, but that's how it's done. Whenever you castle, the king always moves two spaces to the side, and the rook you're castling toward goes to the opposite side of the king.

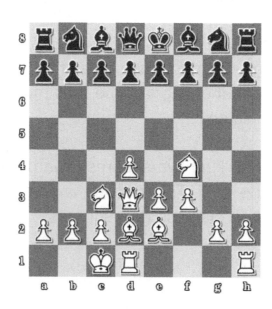

Castling Queenside

This gives the king a safe little fort, or castle to hunker down in. He's safer there, but not completely! Don't trust castling too much!

En Passant

Remember when a pawn can move more than one space in one turn? That's right. On its very first move. This could mean that each pawn has a chance to get out of danger, just like in the diagram below.

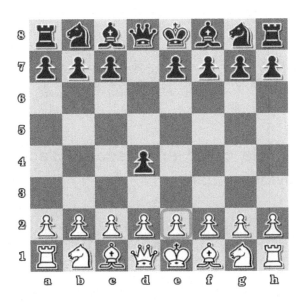

It looks like white's pawn is going to get whacked if it dares to move. But never fear because that pawn hasn't moved yet! So zoom! It moves two spaces on its first go, and now it's safe. Right? Wrong.

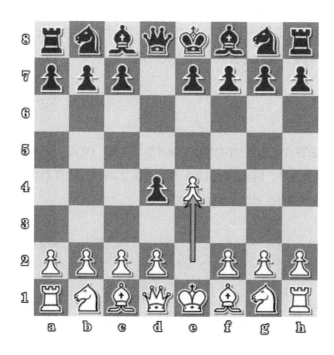

Black decides to use a rule called **en passant.** Black captures the pawn as though it had moved only one square.

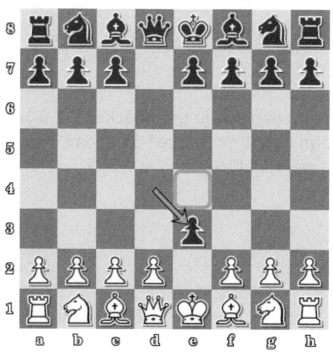

En passant can only be performed by pawns. If black had any other piece, like a bishop, the rule of en passant wouldn't be used.

The next special rule also involves pawns, and it's a rule that most chess players love.

Pawn Promotion

Since pawns can only crawl ahead in one direction, what happens to them when they run out of squares to move in? Like any good veteran that survives a battle, they get a promotion!

If one of your pawns makes it all the way to the other end of the board, then you can convert it to any piece of your choice -- except for a king or a pawn. As a result of this rule, you can have several queens on the board, all in one game. Although sometimes it would be a better idea to make it something other than a queen. But for now, know that it is a good idea to get your pawns to the other side of the board... and it's an even better idea to keep the other player from getting their pawns to your side!

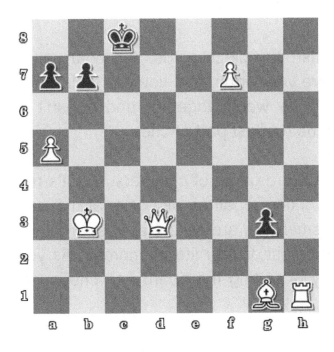

What happens when that f7 pawn makes one last move?

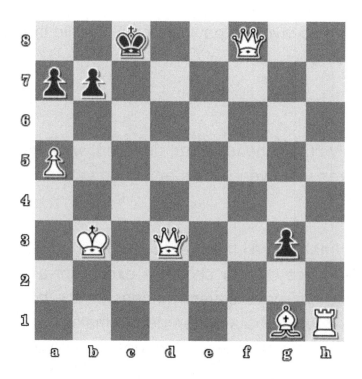

Poof! It's a new queen! Now there are two white queens on the board!

Tactics

It may seem fun to push one piece across the board at a time, but don't forget that your chessmen are your army, and you are their commander. Armies are at their best when everyone works together and doesn't waste time or moves. Learning to do this is the hardest part of chess.

The chessboard looks like a game of checkers. But it's really a battlefield where your chessmen are working together with special moves to win! These special moves that your chessmen use are called **tactics**, and they are the part of chess that you'll be spending most of your life to improve. As you practice, you'll begin to develop a new way of seeing the board -- a chess vision -- and the special moves you can make.

We'll go over these tactics one by one. Don't think that these moves are special to just the pieces shown in the examples. Find ways of performing each tactic with each chessman!

Discovered Attacks

A discovery, or a discovered attack, is a very common tactic in chess. Make no mistake, it is also very powerful! A discovered attack is made when one piece gets out of the way of another, revealing an attack that didn't seem to be of a threat initially. Part of the beauty of a discovery attack is that the piece moving out of the way can do some attacking of its own.

A discovery that threatens a king is called a discovered check. It's not hard to see why.

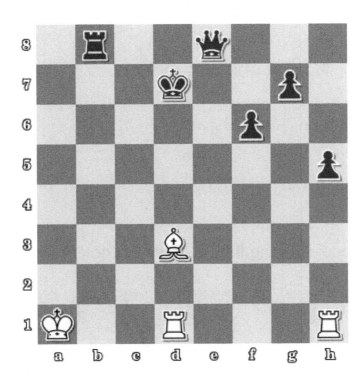

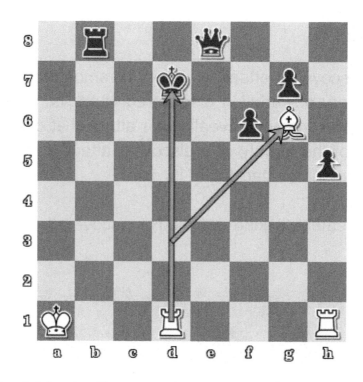

A check on the black king is discovered when the white bishop moves out of the way.

Pins

A pin paralyzes a piece, keeping it from moving. Look at the diagram below.

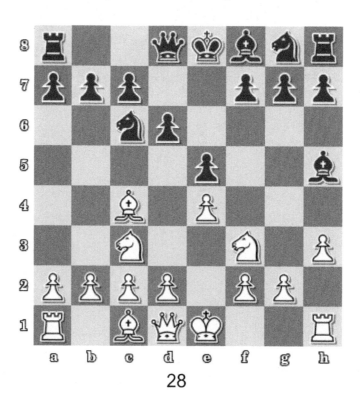

The white knight on f3 is no longer able to help attack the center of the board. Why? Black's bishop on h5 will pounce on the white queen if the knight dares to move a muscle! Thus the knight is **pinned** to where it sits.

Pinning a piece is usually part of a bigger plan. Look at the next diagram.

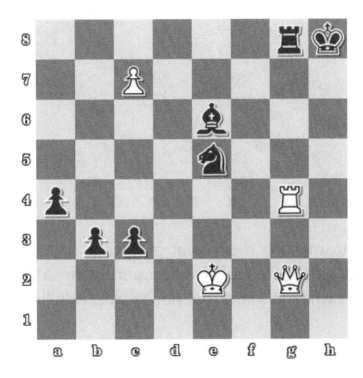

Since white doesn't want to lose their queen, that leaves the rook wide open to attack, and it's got problems coming from several different directions. By pinning a piece, you can make it much easier to capture another piece or that same piece. Pins are especially effective when a king is involved. See the example below.

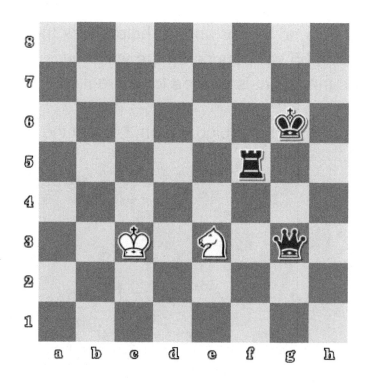

You're not allowed to make a move that puts your own king in check. So the white knight isn't allowed to move! If the queen were in that king's position, it would be a choice for white to make, but not so when it's the king!

Find the Pin 1

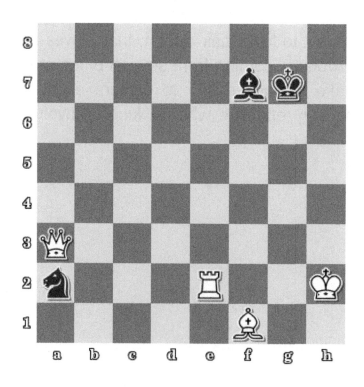

The Bishop on f7 is causing real problems for White since he wants to capture the Knight on a2. How can the Bishop be pinned? That's right!
Qa7.

Forks

The real art of chess comes through in forks. A fork is simply when one piece threatens two or more other pieces at once.

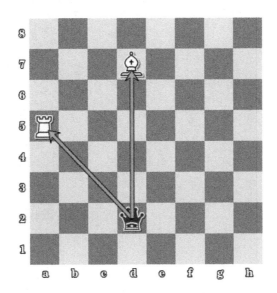

The black queen forks the white rook and the white bishop.

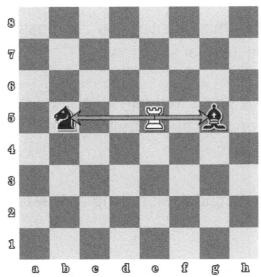

The white rook forks the black knight and the black bishop.

The king of forks is undoubtedly the knight. Other than its ability to breathe fire into 8 squares as well as its ability to jump across other pieces, the knight can also create many "knight-mare" situations involving forks!

Each of black's pieces in this diagram is forked by the white knight. Eight chessmen at once!

You'll probably never see this position on a chessboard, but it shows how powerful the knight can be in ideal situations.

But the knight isn't the only piece that can fork. Her Majesty, the queen, can also threaten eight pieces at once. It's just that with the way she moves, it's not as likely as it is with the knight.

Every other piece is likely to find itself forking at least two other pieces if nobody is careful.

Rooks and bishops can fork very effectively, as shown below. But this power isn't limited to these big and heavy pieces.

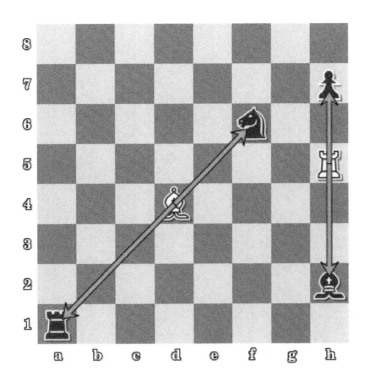

The lowly pawn can fork just fine.

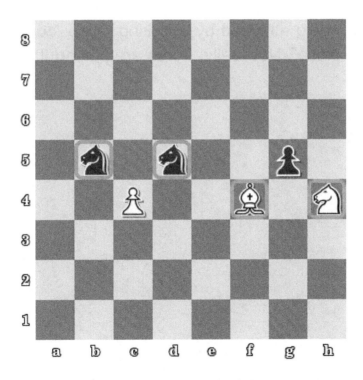

The problem with a fork is that it almost always means that a piece is going to leave the board. This is especially true when a fork involves a check.

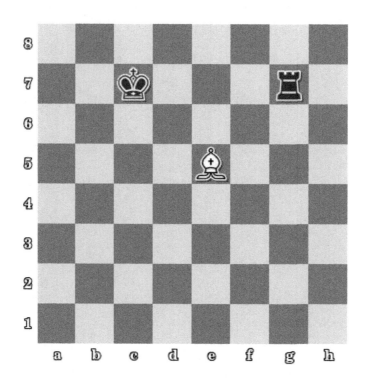

After ..Kb7, black has no choice but to surrender the rook.

So if you're the one being attacked by a forking piece, does that mean that you automatically lose a piece? Not really. Forks are powerful, but they don't always work.

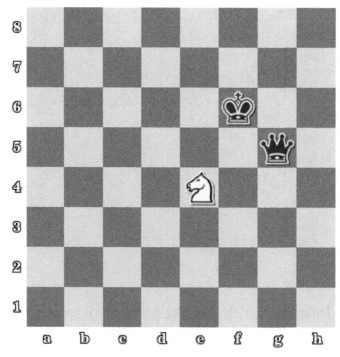

Here the black queen can breathe a sigh of relief since his majesty is close enough to come to the rescue with ...Kf5. But kings aren't medics, and shouldn't be relied on like this. It's much better to prevent forks from happening to you than to get out of one!

Skewers

Is that a funny-looking word? It rhymes with "sewer," just with a k. What a skewer does on the chessboard isn't funny at all. It's a very strong move. It's a pin done in reverse. Pins let you keep an enemy piece from moving. A skewer forces an enemy piece out of the way to capture the one behind it.

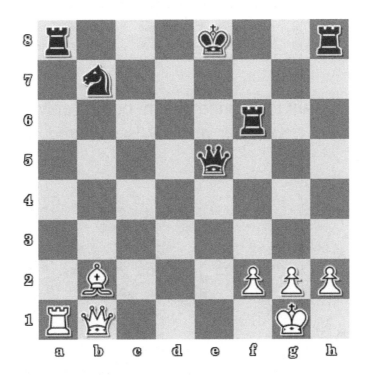

Black doesn't really want to lose their queen just yet. So it is moved to safety with ...Qb5. But the rook behind it is captured! The f6 rook has been skewered!

Skewers often involve checks, since a check forces the king to move.

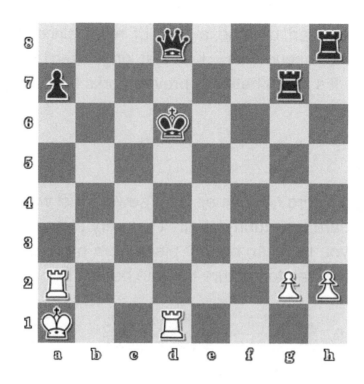

Black certainly doesn't want to lose the queen, but the only way out of check is to move the king. So after ...Ke6, her majesty is captured. The queen has been skewered!

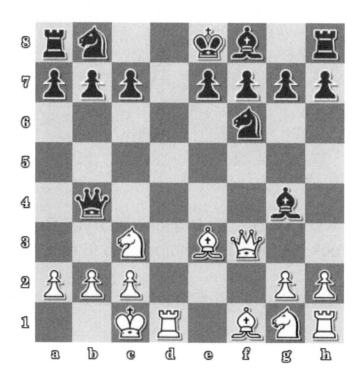

With the black bishop on **g4**, it is attacking both the white's queen and rook. So, I guess you can now see the power of skewer and how black can capture a valuable piece from it.

Sacrifice

A sacrifice in chess is almost the work of an acrobat. It's a risky move that looks like a loss, but one or more moves down the road lead to a gain. Sacrifices rank as one of the great chess thrills.

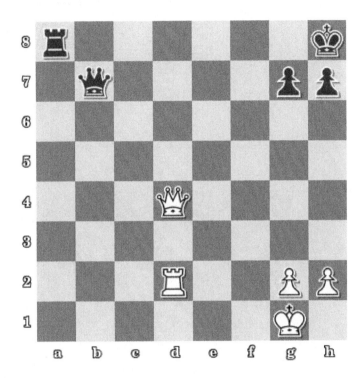

In this position, white decided to play **Qd8+.** This move puts the white queen in danger from the black rook. So why would white do this? Watch what happens.

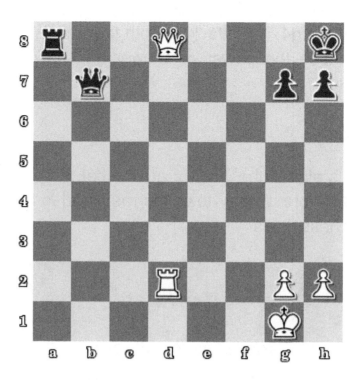

Qd8+

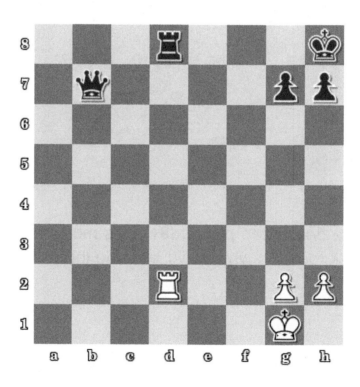

38

..Rxd8

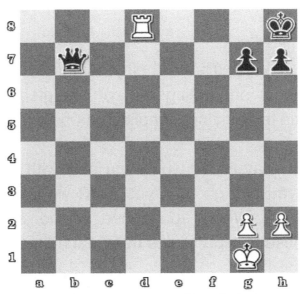

Aha! A checkmate with **Rxd8#.** White **sacrificed** their queen so that they could make this winning move later.

Zugzwang

Chess can be just like life. Sometimes all the moves you can make are moves you don't want to make. When this happens on the chessboard, this is called Zugzwang. That's a very big word, so we'll break it down: ZOOG-shwang. You know you're in zugzwang when every move you can make is a bad move.

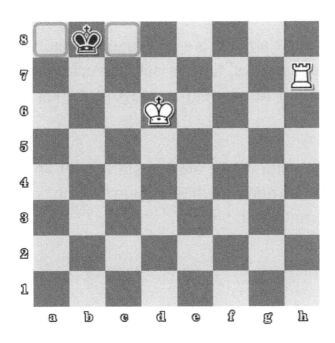

Black is in Zugzwang. Any move that can be made here is a bad move.

Principles of chess

Super serious chess players. That is, players that are planning on entering contests and tournaments and being part of the global chess scene... they devote quite a bit of time to studying complicated openings and diagrams.

What if you just want to play better when you play with your friends? There are four simple principles you can go by if you don't want to memorize a bunch of openings and strategies. When you move on to studying openings and strategies, you'll see these four principles used each time.

They are:

- **Time**
- **Space**
- **Force**
- **Pawn Structure**

We're going to look at each one individually.

Time

From the beginning of the game, there is a race to victory. Even if you're playing without one of the chess clocks, time is still a crucial part of the game, and it's measured in who is going to be able to move out their pieces and make their plans work the fastest.

Since white always goes first, white always starts with an advantage in time, and black has to find ways of getting white to waste time, or waste moves so that black can steal the advantage in time.

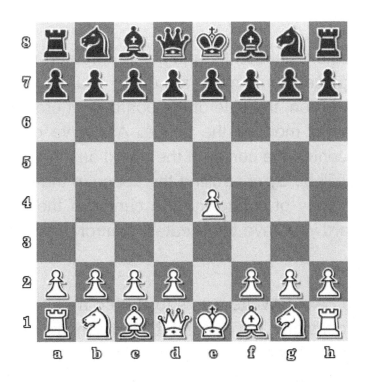

Since white always goes first, white starts with an advantage in time.

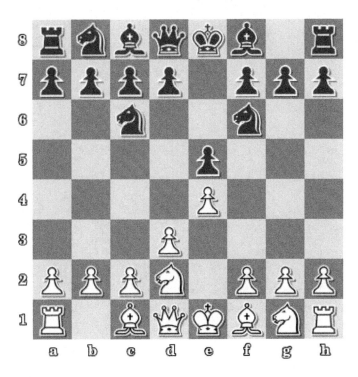

By making moves that force white to play defensively, black can steal that advantage in time.

41

Space

It's one thing to threaten pieces. It's another to threaten squares. The squares where each of your pieces could move are under your control. This is the **space** that you control. In addition, the side of the board is where you gain the greatest advantage in controlling most of the space. As we've discussed earlier, you would want to try to control the center of the board as much as possible. If not by occupying it, then it will be by controlling the space in the center of the board. If you don't have the luxury of controlling the center of the board, then examine which part of the board you have the greatest control of space in, then plan from there.

Look at the example below. White wants to launch an attack. Which side of the board should white focus on? That's right! It's the right side of the board. Most of the squares are being stared down by the bishops and the knights. If Black wants to attack from that side, he's going to have a very difficult time doing it.

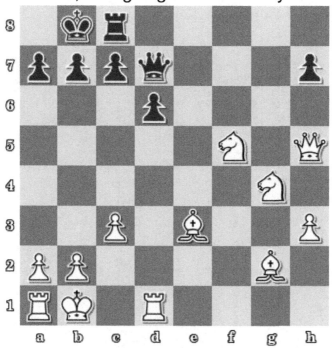

Force

Force is similar to space. With space, you look at squares that are empty but under your control. The principle of force is governed by where your pieces are concentrated.

In the diagram below, black has most of his forces active on the KQ side of the board, so it makes sense that he would want to launch his attack or execute his plans from there. White has slightly less force on the same side, but his rooks are open and barreling down the other side of the board. These are things for him to consider before he decides which side of the board to plan his attack.

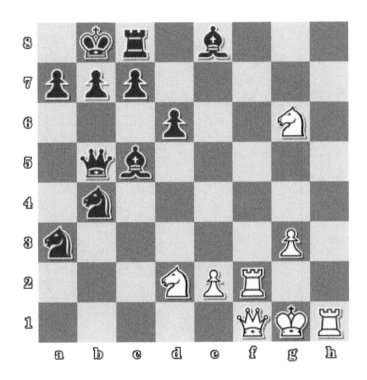

Which side of the board should black use to stage an attack?

43

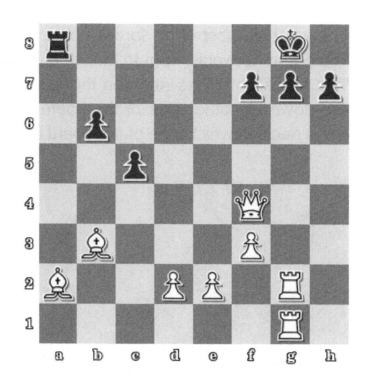

White would want to mount an attack from the kingside of the board since that is where most of his force is.

Pawn Structure

Those pawns. They're slow. They seem to get in the way. How much would the game actually depend on them? More than you might think at first. For, to quote the Chessmaster Philidor:

...to play the pawns well; they are the soul of chess: it is they which uniquely determine the attack and the defense, and on their good or bad arrangement depends entirely the winning or losing of the game.

Pawns look like they're a dime a dozen. But they can form some very important formations and structures on the chessboard. They are known as the following:

- **Pawn chains**
- **Passed pawns**
- **Backward pawns**

- **Pawn Islands**
- **Hanging Pawns/Phalanx pawns**
- **Isolated Pawns**

Pawn Chains

A pawn chain can be said simply to be several pawns placed diagonally from each other, as seen in the diagram. A pawn chain is actually a very powerful thing to have, as it helps you control space on the board and creates some safe staging areas for pieces like knights and bishops. Like everything else in chess, some weaknesses go along with strengths. Notice that each pawn chain controls only one color of squares. The opposite color of squares are potential weak spots for the enemy to exploit.

You also need to realize that the squares occupied by the pawn chain can cramp movement for friend and foe alike. This is especially true for bishops. However nice White's pawn chain is, it makes life difficult for one of the two bishops.

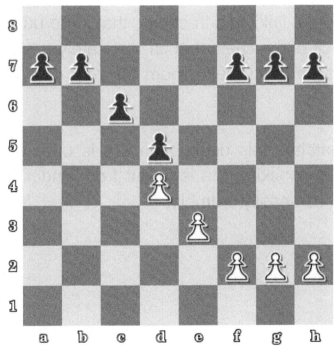

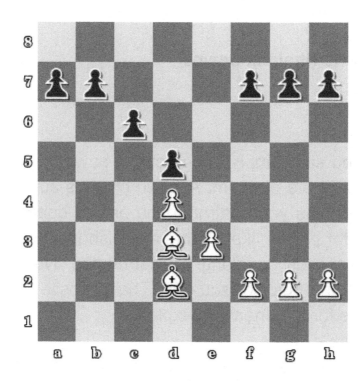

The pawn chain blocks one bishop but frees the other.

Backward Pawns

Every chain has a weak link, and in chess, that's the backward pawn. It's the pawn at the very back of the chain that cannot safely advance. This makes it a prime target to take down to make room for your own pieces in the enemy camp.

Note that it only matches this description if it is unable to advance without being threatened. By knocking the legs out from under the backward pawn, the rest of the chain can easily crumble.

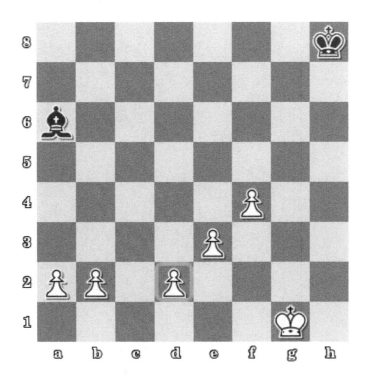

The d2 pawn has no protection if it advances, so it is a backward pawn.

Pawn Islands

Neither good nor bad, pawn islands describe the groups of pawns that are on the board without a link to the other pawns. Take a look at the diagram below. White has two pawn islands, while black has three. Yes, a pawn island can consist of only one pawn. Generally speaking, the fewer pawn islands you have, the better. That way, there's less room for enemy pieces to make their nests. But that also means there is less room for your own pieces to move out.

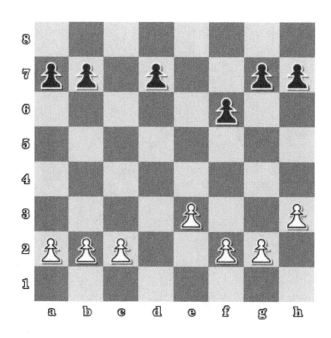

Isolated Pawns

A pawn that has no other friendly pawns in the files next to it has become an isolated pawn. These can be very expensive for you to protect if you insist on keeping them. The square right in front of an isolated pawn is the perfect place for a piece to anchor itself.

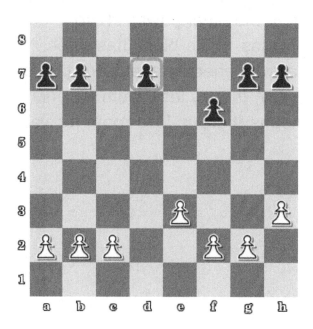

The d7 pawn is an isolated pawn.

Phalanx Pawns

A pawn phalanx occurs when two or more pawns stand beside each other in files. This pawn structure is both strong and weak. It is strong because the squares in front of them form a solid wall of space that enemy pieces cannot stand in without worry. But this formation is also weak because the pawns are unable to protect each other. Other pawns or pieces will have to be drafted into the job of protecting the phalanx, and that isn't always ideal. Since this formation is all attack and no defense, it is sometimes referred to as hanging pawns.

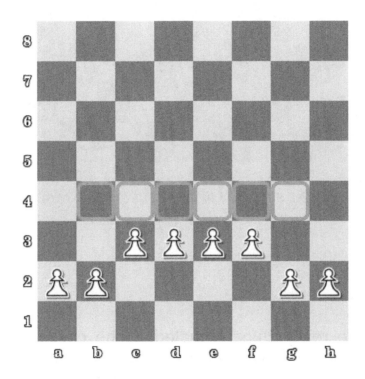

A pawn phalanx creates a wall of protected space, but only two of the four pawns are defended.

Passed Pawns

The name doesn't sound very good, but passed pawns are actually a very good thing. A passed pawn is a pawn that cannot be stopped from advancing to the end rank where it can be promoted.

By now, you would have noticed that the section on pawn structure is the longest. It goes to show how you cannot underestimate how important the pawns are in chess. They seem weak and unimportant, and yet they can decide the direction of the game.

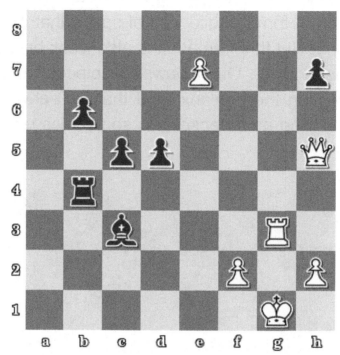

The pawn on e7 cannot be stopped from reaching the last row or rank. So it is a passed pawn.

Chess openings

Now it's time for the really crunchy material. The chess game is divided into three parts; the opening, the midgame, and the endgame. In this section, we are going to focus on the opening. It will be impossible to cover every single detail of chess openings in this book. There are at least 1,327 documented chess openings and variants, or different ways of performing those openings. That doesn't even cover the variants that players themselves have come up with.

With all that variety, openings fall into two basic camps. There are openings that lead to open and wild tactical play with fireworks alongside bold fast moves and quick strikes. And then, there are openings that lead to slow, cramped games that force each player to crawl across the board through tight muddy passages. The opening you use will depend on what you like and how your opponent tries to steer the game. Both ways of playing can be fun, and learning to play both ways can be a form of strategy in the game. If you can tell that the other player likes a lot of action and a game that doesn't drag on forever, playing a closed and cramped game will get your opponent to become impatient and make careless moves, which will help you win. They may even try to make an open game out of a closed game, which will also give you the advantage.

The opposite is true. If your opponent likes the closed games, then steering things into an open and tactical game will throw them out of their comfortable playing style, where they will have to deal with fire coming at them from all over the board.

So it's safe to say that you should know a little bit about both styles of play, even if you have a favorite. First, we'll look at more open games, and then we'll look at the closed and cramped ones.

Open Games: Fast and Furious

Open games happen when the pawns in the center files move out soon, and the paths of pieces like bishops and the queen are opened up quickly. The center pawns are often traded off early, which opens up the board to all kinds of bombs, bullets, and cannonballs.

The most popular of all open games is:

1. e4

Remember what we learned about recording chess games? This means that on White's first move, the pawn on the E file moves to the 4th rank; e4. It is simply called **The King's Pawn Game** when it starts off with this move.

This has been an extremely popular opening in both serious and friendly games. It gets the pieces of both sides out quickly and usually makes for a quick game full of action and surprises where nobody has time to get bored.

But don't forget that it takes two to tango. Black will have to make moves that lead to an open game also. **1. e4** gives black a chance to turn the game into one of the slowest and most cramped games ever with **1. ... c5**, or the pawn on the c file moving to the 5th rank. This begins the **Sicilian Defense**.

If Black is in the spirit of an open game, then they will play **1...e5**, which begins the **Ruy Lopez,** or **Spanish Game.** After a series of book moves such as

1.e4 e5
2.Nf3 Nc6
3.Bb5

We find ourselves with the following position:

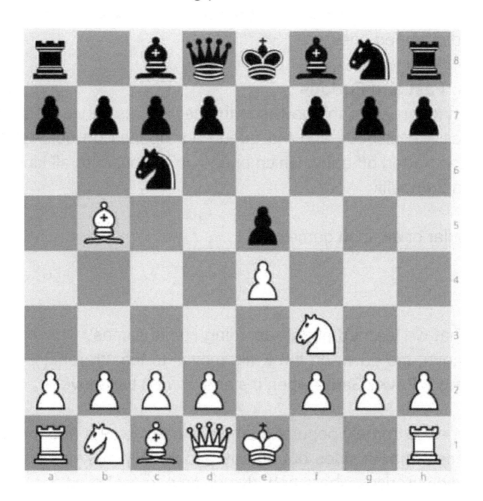

The Ruy Lopez is a fantastic chess opening for beginners. Not only does it (usually) lead to the fun of open games, it gets white into a good position soon, and black also has a fair shot at tilting things in his favor as well. At this stage, things look pretty decent for white. His knight and his pawn both stab solidly into the center of the board while the b5 bishop is already looking to remove the black pawn's protector from c6. Not only that, the white king will also be able to castle away to safety almost immediately.

But there is so much room for possibilities with this chess opening. Here at this point, neither side has lost any material.

From here, the opening splinters into many different directions. There's an **Exchange variation** where white lets go of some material to better his position.

After the last **3.Bb5,** black tries to send the bishop home with **3...a6**

This leads to **4.Bxc6 dxc6** with this result:

- Positional Play: Cramped and Crowded

Whereas games starting with e4 lead to dramatic performances on open fields, opening moves that lead to closed midgames are much more like squeezing through a maze or a cavern.

One of the most popular openings leading to a closed position is **The Sicilian Defense.** It opens as follows

1. e4 c5

From this point on, there are plenty of different ways to go with the Sicilian. Enough to keep you studying for most of your life. The Sicilian not only sets up black with a solid set of defenses, but it also encourages white to waste a move, causing black to gain an advantage in **time**, as we discussed earlier in the four basic principles of playing chess. If white wastes a move and black make moves that help develop black's position, then black gains an advantage.

The **Dragon Variation** of The Sicilian continues as follows:

1. Nf3 d6
2. d4 cxd4
3. Nxd4 Nf6
4. Nc3 g6

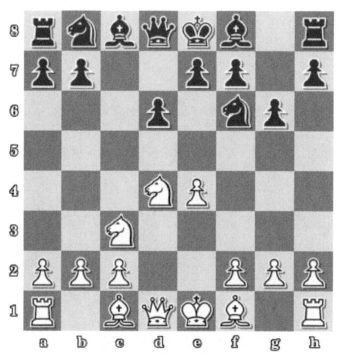

Look at the numerous options black now has. The f8 bishop can snipe at the center of the board from g7. The queen and the c8 bishop have room to breathe. No wonder the Dragon Variation is a popular defense for black.

- Developing Your Position

If you do not yet want to work with a specific chess opening, that is fine. Try to focus on moving each chess piece only once in the beginning. If you can afford to ignore threats to your side of the board, then ignore them so that you don't give the other side an advantage in time and development. Things happen quickly in the beginning of chess. Everything that each player does in the beginning will come back to haunt them later in the mid- and endgame.

That also means that if you can develop your pieces in such a way that also threatens your opponent's position, do it. That way, you're doing two jobs at once: Developing and setting up your position on the board while making it difficult or impossible for the other side to do the same. This simultaneously gives you advantages in **time, space, and force.**

Chess Middle Game

When does the opening end and the middle game begin? Nobody really knows. But it's at a point when both sides have traded off some pawns and maybe some pieces and there's room on the board to start making long-range plans and most of the pieces have been moved from their starting positions.

The middle game is often the hardest part for many players. In the opening of the game, you can execute some moves from memory. You can simply make sure that you don't touch the same piece twice. In the endgame, as we'll see later, you're looking for ways to checkmate the other king.

But in the middle game, it's a wide-open field of possibilities. There are no memorized moves and tricks to help out here. It really is up to the player to develop plans and try to guess what his opponent is going to try to do. Here is where your "chess vision," your ability to calculate, will really develop like a muscle used constantly.

That said, there are some principles to keep in mind when voyaging into the wild battlefield of the middle game.

- Controlling Space

Controlling space is especially an active principle of chess in the middle game. Space that is controlled is simply space that won't be used by the opposition, and it's always a rude surprise when an attack comes from a direction that nobody was paying attention to!

No two games will ever be the same, but there are some parts of the board that certain pieces have an advantage on. By the time you reach the middle game, you will want to have those pieces in or around those places.

- Fianchettoed Bishops

Like all your other pieces, your bishops will do their job the best if they're located towards the center of the board. What if that's just not a possibility? The next best thing is to try to get your bishops in control of either diagonal line that runs through the center of the board.

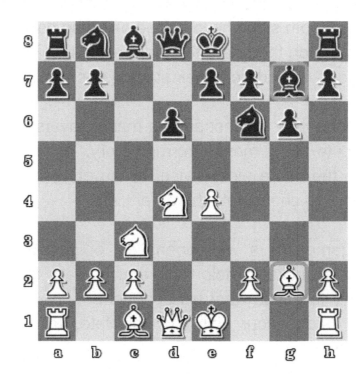

Both bishops in this example are fianchettoed.

Like a long-range sniper, the bishop can control a great deal of space that will allow him to pick off would-be squatters in the board's center. This is why some chess openings move the bishops on to these lines as early as possible. This move of the bishop is known as a fianchetto.

- Keeping the action in the center of the board

Just as it was the case at the beginning of the game, so it is the case in the middle game: You want to try to keep the action towards the center of the board. This isn't a hard and fast rule, but if you can't keep your pieces around the center of the board, you can at least try to capture toward the center of the board. This puts the spaces that your pieces threaten close to the center. Remember what we said about knights? Where are they the strongest? That's right—the center of the board.

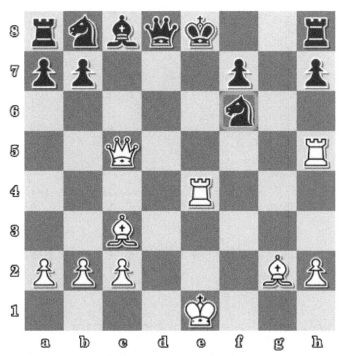

Our knight has a choice of pieces to capture in a powerful fork. There's a saying in chess about knights. "A knight on the rim is dim." This means that you mostly want to try to move your knights away from the far sides of the board. There are a few times this isn't true, though. As we've said repeatedly that there are exceptions to every rule. This isn't one of those times. Our knight gains a decided advantage when he captures closer to the center of the board, raining down fire in a wide circle that everyone is going to have to tiptoe around on the cramped sides of the board.

Move Your Rooks to Open Files

Don't forget that your rooks are like long-range cannons. The more squares in front of them, the farther they fire. Or rather, the more space they can control. In the diagram below, one rook can make an easy and simple move to gain a huge control of space on the board. What move do you think it would be?

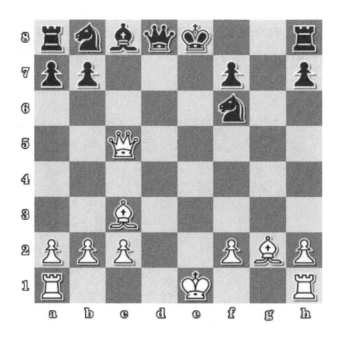

If you said **Rd1,** you were right! The other one is locked in and won't be that useful anytime soon.

The next best thing you can do is to double up your rooks on a single file. This creates a battering ram that is very difficult to stop. It has led to many a checkmate. To have both rooks and the queen on the same file is devastating to whoever is going to be on the receiving end.

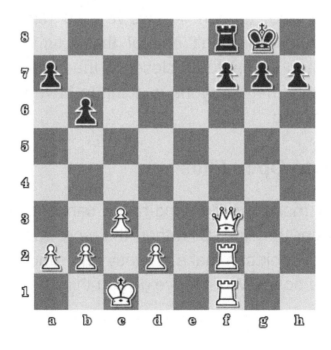

Keep Both Bishops

More often than not, having both bishops is more useful than having both knights. Aside from the sheer force that comes from having both bishops, they serve as two sides of the same coin, since one will only be able to attack light-colored squares and the other will only be able to attack dark-colored squares. The example below shows the firepower that comes from keeping the pair.

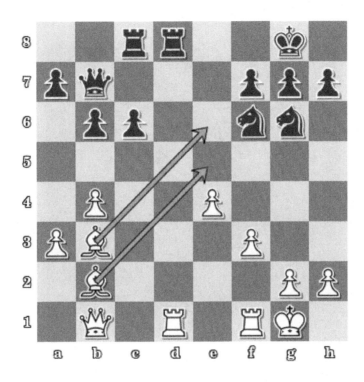

That's a double-layered fence that will be difficult to get through.

Trade Your Flank Pawns for Center Pawns

You wouldn't think there would be much to do with your pawns in the middle game other than push them forward, but they too offer you a chance to gain space and control in the all-important center of the board. If you have pawns in the center files, such as the d-file and the e-file, try to keep them there. However, if you get a chance to trade off your flank pawns (pawns toward the sides of the board) closer to the *e* and *f* files, by all means, do so! These pawns will later be able to create chances to guard and anchor down positions for knights and others in the center.

Avoid Creating Weak Squares In Your Position

A weak square is a square that cannot be protected by a pawn on your side of the board. These squares are perfect outposts for the enemy to land on and take over. If a weak square is close to your king or the center of the board, then you've got a lot of trouble waiting to happen.

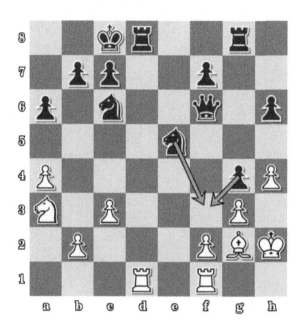

That f3 square may not be unguarded, but it paralyzes white's bishop into guard duty. Not only that, but it's being attacked twice and defended only once. It's only a matter of time before black turns it into an outpost in the white king's backyard that will lead to a checkmate.

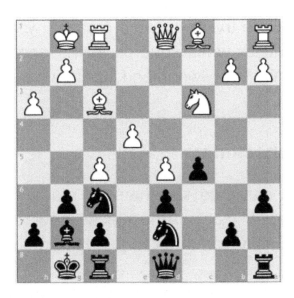

White just played f4-f5 and created a whole world of problems for himself. It instantly created a home for black's knight as it travels via Ne5 and puts the question to the bishop about how badly it wants to stay in business.

It pays to look for weak squares even when things are crowded. Hidden in this tangled jungle are two places that white's c3 knight could build a nest without much trouble. Yes, there's a black bishop eyeing those squares, but any capture could be retaliated against by the c4 or e4 pawns.

At the same time that you're trying to avoid creating weak squares in your own camp, be on the lookout for weak squares in the enemy camp. They're very comfortable places for knights to swoop and create a safe space for more of your men.

Endgame: How to checkmate

The endgame is a little easier to see than the move from the opening to the middle game. By this point, most of the pieces have been removed from the board. The kings can usually come out to join the fight with the threats to their well-being reduced.

As you can see, the king can take a very active role in the fight against the opposite king, even playing a part in the achievement of a checkmate. So the king's newfound usefulness still carries with it the need for a certain level of caution: Both sides are actively looking for a path to a checkmate.

The paths to a checkmate are often one or two steps ahead. Often there are barriers and defenders to putting down the other king, and this is where plans and tactics are especially necessary. Here are a few examples of what a good checkmate looks like.

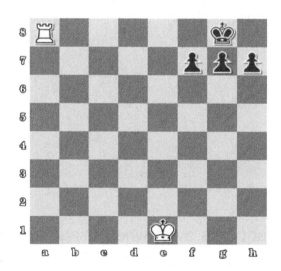

This example is a sobering reminder that a checkmate doesn't have to be complicated.

Which king is in checkmate here?

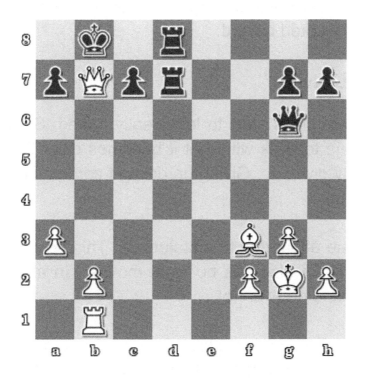

Why can't the lone white queen be captured?

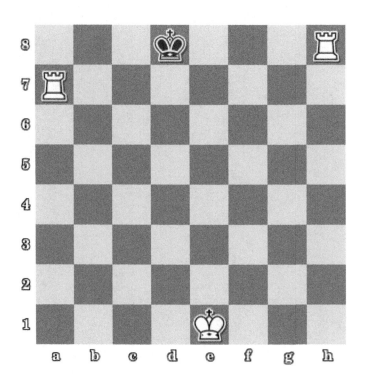

Why can't the black king go anywhere safe?

As mentioned, these positions didn't present themselves on their own. They had to be uncovered and worked toward.

How Games are Drawn

By the endgame, both sides start to look really naked. Sometimes there is so little left for either side to work with that it becomes clear that nobody will really win unless somebody gives up. Giving up doesn't come naturally to a competitor in a chess tournament.

A draw can also come about due to a stalemate. This occurs when the player to move is not in check but also has no legal moves. In all other instances, the players have a choice to draw or not.

Good and bad manners come into play when it comes to offering and accepting a draw. After you play your move, you can simply say, "I offer a draw."

If you're the one being offered the draw, then you simply shake hands with the other player if you accept. Otherwise, you make your own move and say that you would like to play on.

Learning From Past Games

There are plenty of courses out there that promise to make you a better chess player. You know what? Many of them will. But they will also cost a lot of money.

One of the best ways of learning shouldn't cost much or anything at all. Find a database of past games. These are very easy to find, and they often include games from very early, including the 1800s.

What you're going to do is pick a side and try to guess that side's next move on each move. Then look to see what the actual move was. If you guessed the next move correctly, good and well. But if you didn't, try to see why. Just because you didn't guess the player's next move right, it doesn't mean that the player made the best possible move. Many chess databases are full of notes by others on what could have gone differently or better if a player decided to do something else. But for the most part, this will teach you how to make logical moves in chess without spending a fortune on lessons. Let's study one of these games together.

Here is a match between the legendary Paul Morphy and a No Name player called NN in the record. The fun part about this game is that Morphy was only 11 years old. The year was 1848.

1.e4 e5

2.h3

Paul Morphy vs NN
New Orleans (1848), New Orleans, LA USA
King Pawn Game: General (C20) · 1-0

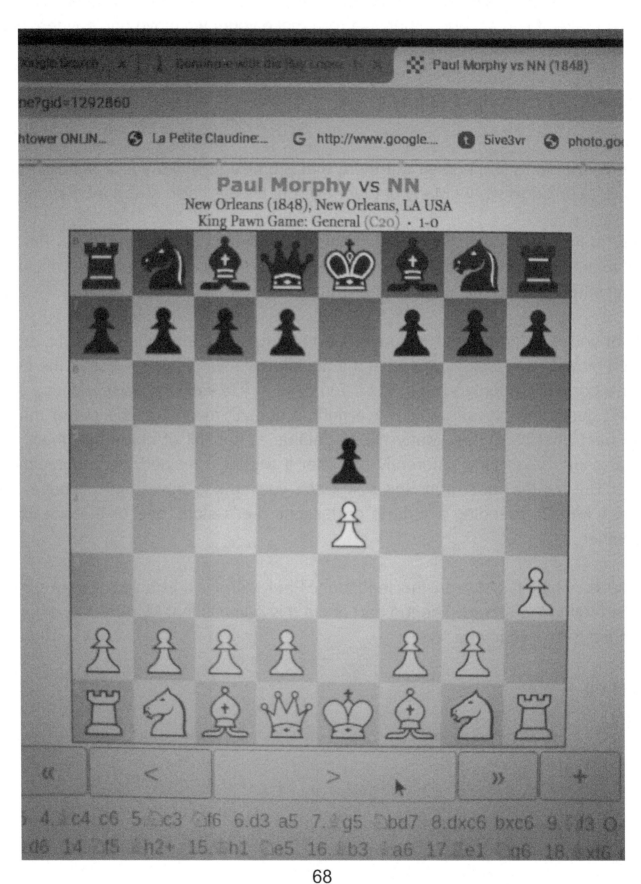

«   <   >   »   +

4. c4 c6 5.♘c3 ♘f6 6.d3 a5 7.♗g5 ♘bd7 8.dxc6 bxc6 9.♘f3 O-
d6 14.♘f5 ♕h2+ 15.♔h1 ♘e5 16.♗b3 ♗a6 17.♖e1 ♘g6 18. xf6

This seems like a very peculiar move. Either Morphy was deliberately offering NN the center of the board, or Morphy was just a kid. We'll never know.

Your author over here personally guessed a move more like 2.Nf3 or even 2.d3. But no. Little Morphy had plans of his own.

2...d5

3.exd5 Bc5

Does it seem strange that black let that white pawn sit in the center of the board? Something more like 3...Qxd5 might seem more called for. This gets the queen out into the action, and black dominates the center of the board. But the move still makes sense because after 3...Qxd5, white can more than buy back the lost time with 4.Nc3, threatening her majesty and causing black to lose time with wasting moves. Possibly more than one. After 4...Qd7, 5.Bb5 harasses the queen again, and black loses more time. Maybe Morphy knew what he was doing with 2.h3 after all...

4.Bc4 c6

5.Nc3 Nf6

6.d3 a5

7.Bg5 Nbd7

8.dxc6 bxc6

9.Nf3 O-O

10.O-O h6

11.Bh4 Qc7

12.d4 exd4

13.Nxd4 Bd6

14.Nf5 Bh2+

15.Kh1 Ne5

16.Bb3 Ba6

17.Re1 Ng6

18.Bxf6 gxf6

19.Qh5 1-0

Parting Words

If you've really read this far in this book along with studying the examples, then you have really come a long way!

What do you think? Do you love chess more than you did when you started this book? Are you fired up to learn more about the game and how to open and end it?

Whatever you do in chess, do it for the love of the game first. If you're trying to become the person that knows everything about chess, you will be unhappy. *Nobody* knows everything about chess. Even grandmasters lose games to people that know less than they do.

Fame in chess comes slowly, and with some of the hardest work that you'll ever do. If you're playing chess just to become famous, you might want to save yourself some trouble and find an easier way to become famous.

Play chess because you love it first. Then play it for all the other reasons.

Made in the USA
Coppell, TX
03 December 2020

42965193R00044